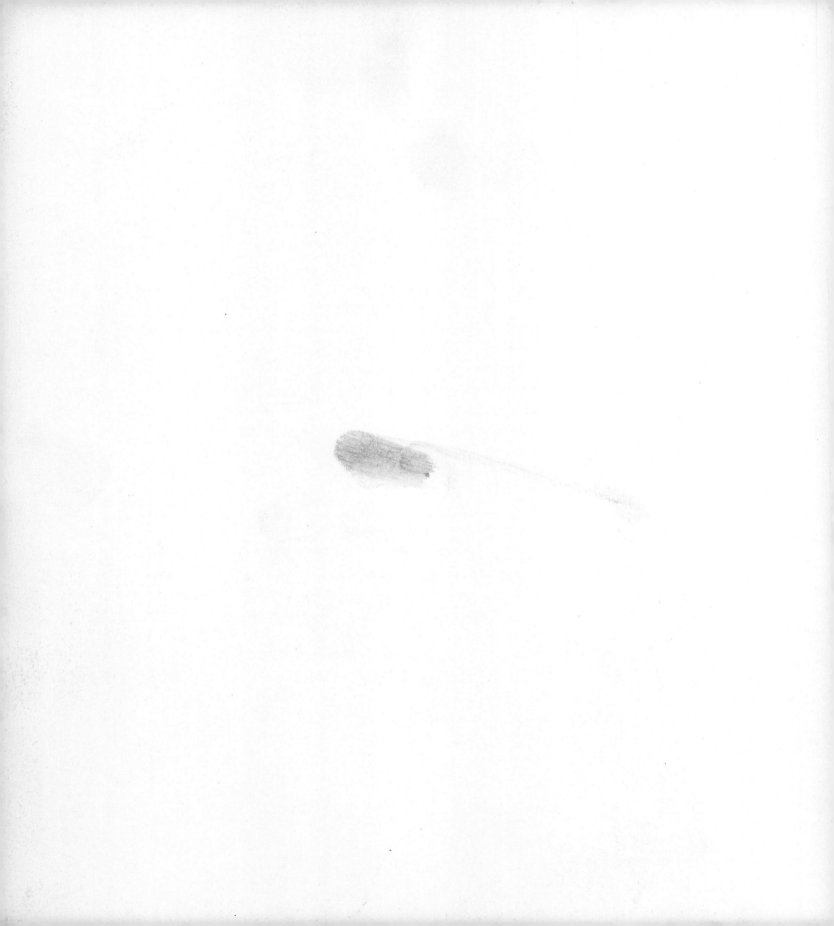

This book belongs to:

Quarto is the authority on a wide range of topics.

Quarto educates, entertains and enriches the lives of our readers—enthusiasts and lovers of hands-on living.

www.quartoknows.com

© 2018 Quarto Publishing plc

First Published in 2018 by QEB Publishing,
an imprint of The Quarto Group.
6 Orchard Road, Suite 100,
Lake Forest, CA 92630
T: +1 949 380 7510
F: +1 949 380 7575
www.QuartoKnows.com

A CIP record for this book is available
from the Library of Congress.

ISBN 978 1 68297 306 6

Manufactured in Dongguan, China TL112017

9 8 7 6 5 4 3 2 1

Author: Su Box
Illustrator: Simona Sanfilippo
Editorial Director: Vicky Garrard
Designer: Victoria Kimonidou

Stories Jesus Told Us

CONTENTS

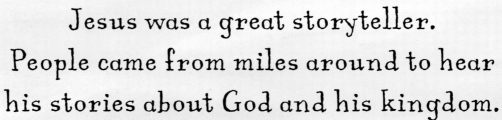

Jesus was a great storyteller.
People came from miles around to hear
his stories about God and his kingdom.

His stories were about ordinary
things, but they made people
think and ask questions.

One day as the crowd listened, Jesus pointed to a farmer in a nearby field.

People turned to look. The man was sowing
seeds as he walked up and down the field.

Jesus told them this
story about a sower...

"One evening, a farmer said, 'The field is ready. It's time to plant my crops.'

12

Early next morning, he filled a big bag with grain seeds, slung it over his shoulder, and set off to his field.

"Slowly and steadily, the farmer trudged up and down the plowed field.

Handful by handful, he threw seeds into the air.

Whoosh!

14

Where did the scattered seeds fall?

15

"Some seeds landed nearby.
Others were carried away by the breeze.

The little seeds fell here and there...
the farmer didn't notice where.

He would find out
when the seeds
grew shoots.

17

"Some seeds fell on the footpath
where people trod on them...

CRUNCH!

CRUNCH!

18

...and then greedy birds swooped down and gobbled them up!

CAW!

CAW!

"Some seeds fell on stony ground.

The seeds began to grow, but they
needed water. Soon their tiny shoots
drooped and died in the hot sun.

Some seeds fell among thorns.
The seeds put down roots and grew
strong shoots. But the thorns were
stronger and choked the little plants.

21

"But some seeds fell on good rich soil. They made deep roots and grew big green shoots.

The farmer was pleased to see these strong new plants.

'Maybe the harvest will
be good,' he said.

"At last harvest-time came.

'It's time to cut the crop!'
said the farmer.

WHEW!

He and his helpers worked all day
to harvest the golden ears of wheat.

24

And every plant made lots of new seeds—a hundred times more than the seed the farmer had sown."

"But what does the story mean?"
asked one of Jesus' friends.

"The seeds are what
God tells us about his
kingdom," said Jesus.
"Some people don't really
listen. So God's message
is snatched away, like the
seeds the birds gobbled up.

"Some people are glad to
hear what God tells them.
But as soon as trouble
comes, they are just like
the plants that drooped
and died.

"Some people hear and gladly accept God's teaching. Then their life gets too busy and their understanding does not grow. That's like the seeds that fell among thorns.

"But some people really listen and understand what God wants.

28

"They are like the seeds that fell on good soil and the plants that made more new seeds.

"They do as God asks and their lives show amazing results."

29

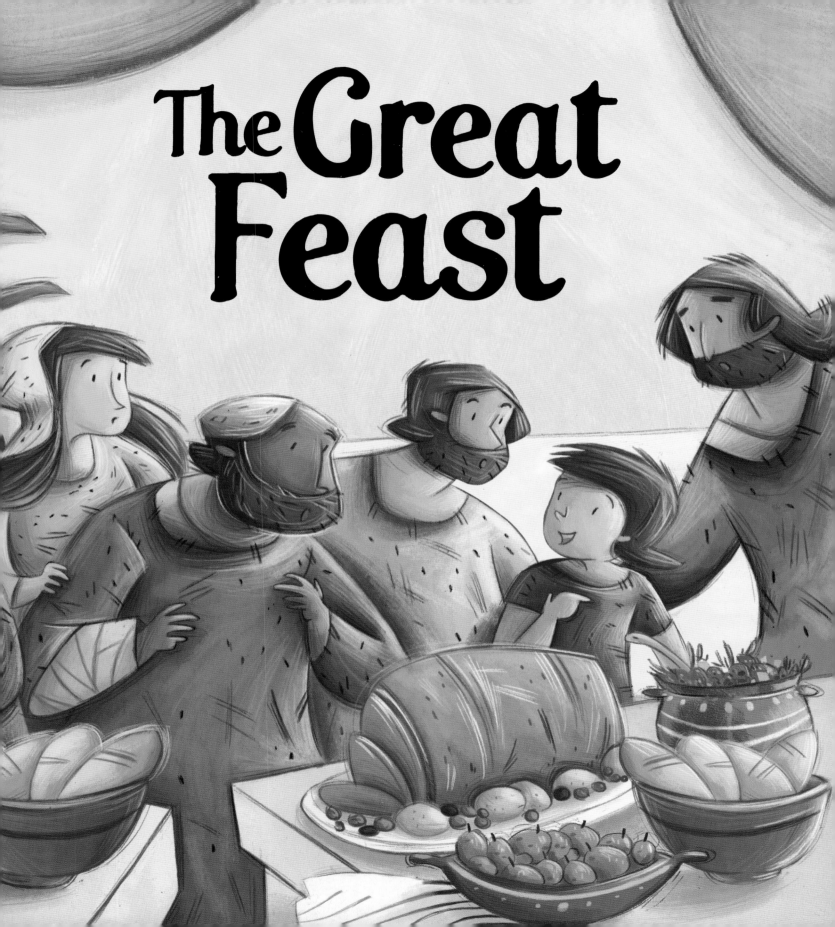

The Great Feast

One day, Jesus was at a party.
All the guests thought they were
important or special. But they
didn't live as God wanted, so
Jesus told this story.

32

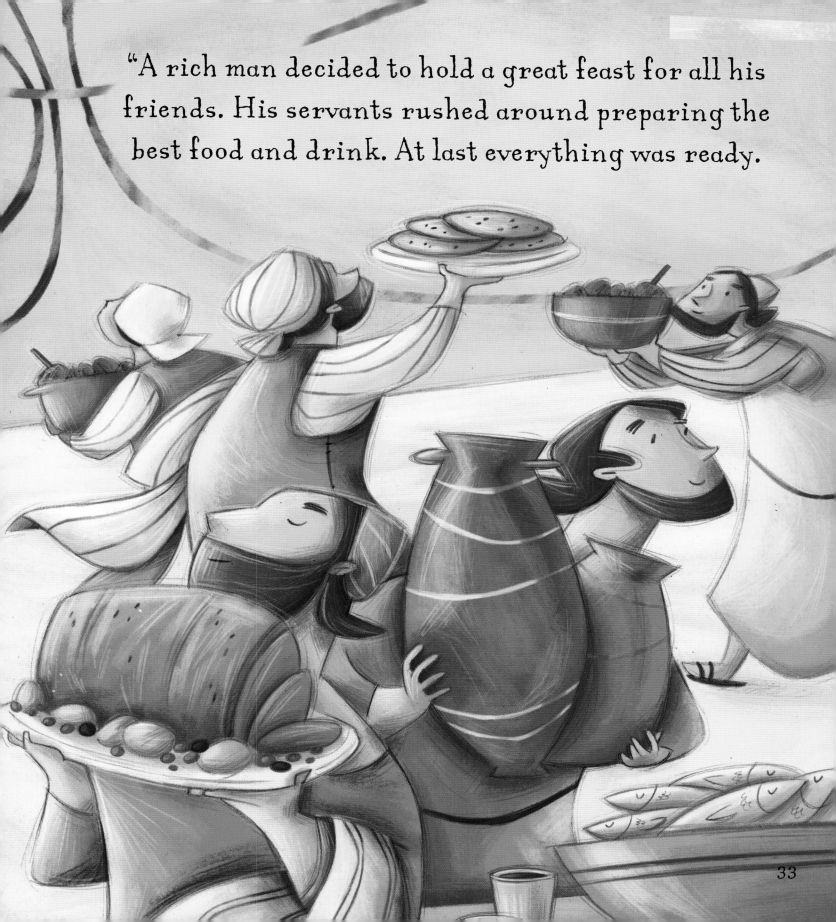

"A rich man decided to hold a great feast for all his friends. His servants rushed around preparing the best food and drink. At last everything was ready.

"The rich man's servant went to tell the invited guests that the feast was ready.

But they were all busy with less important things.

The servant came back and said,
'Your guests could not come.
Each one made an excuse...'

35

"'I've just bought some land. I'm too busy.'

'I've just bought some oxen. I'm too busy.'

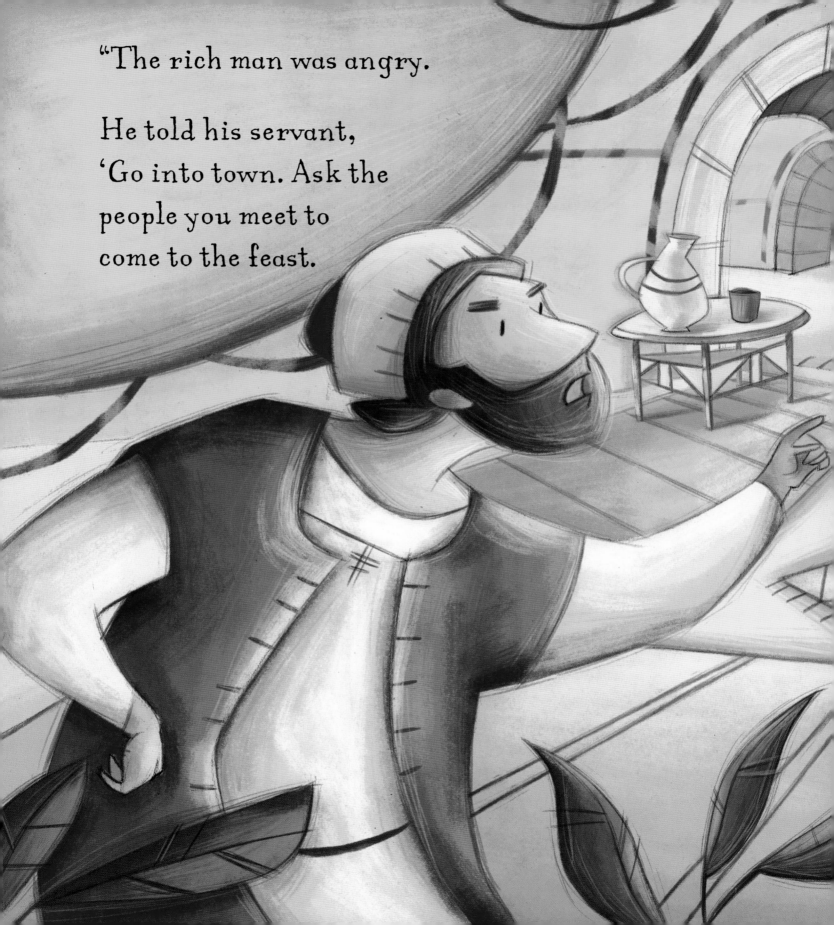

"The rich man was angry.

He told his servant, 'Go into town. Ask the people you meet to come to the feast.

'Look for the poor, and the sick, and people without a home.

Invite them to my party.'

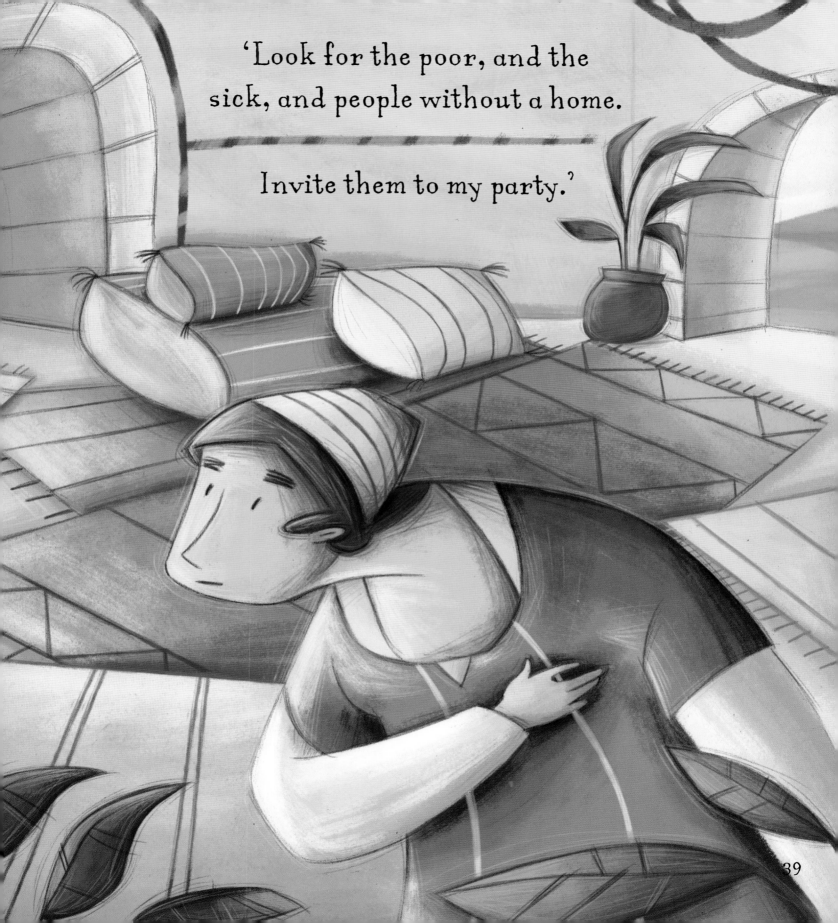

"The servant did just that.

Soon ragged and hungry people crowded into the big house.

40

But there was room
for more guests.

"The rich man sent the servant out again.

'Go into the countryside. Look
for any tramps or needy people.

42

'Invite them so that my house will be full.'

"The rich man said,
'Anyone who wants to eat,
let them come and take a seat.'

He had asked people
who didn't usually get
invited anywhere.

45

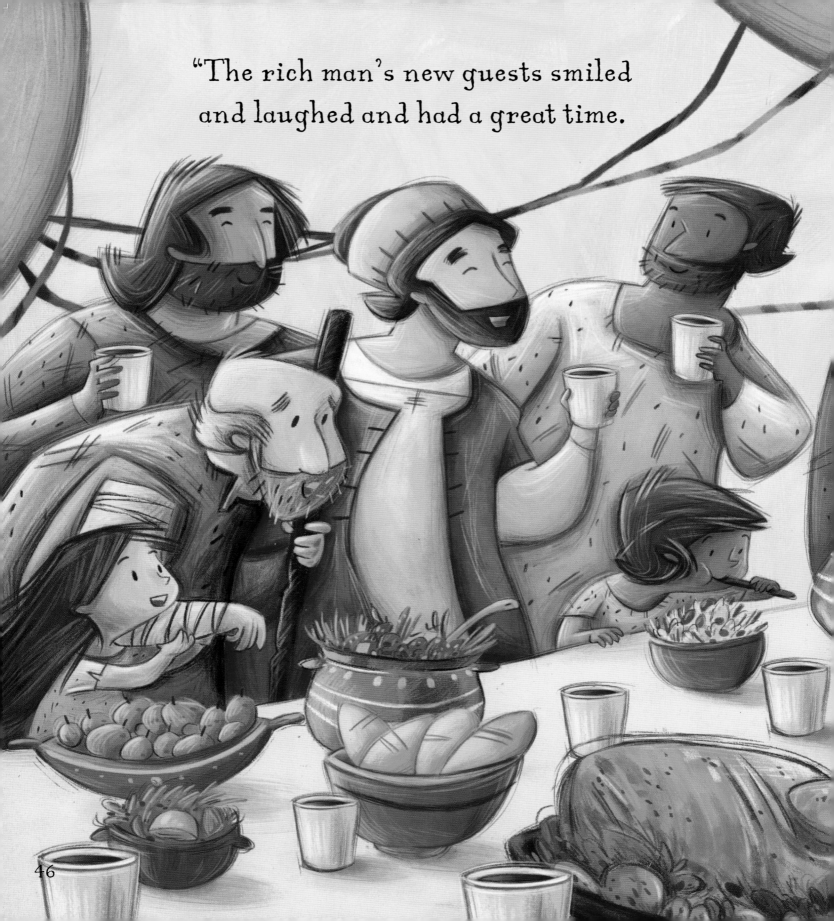

"The rich man's new guests smiled and laughed and had a great time.

46

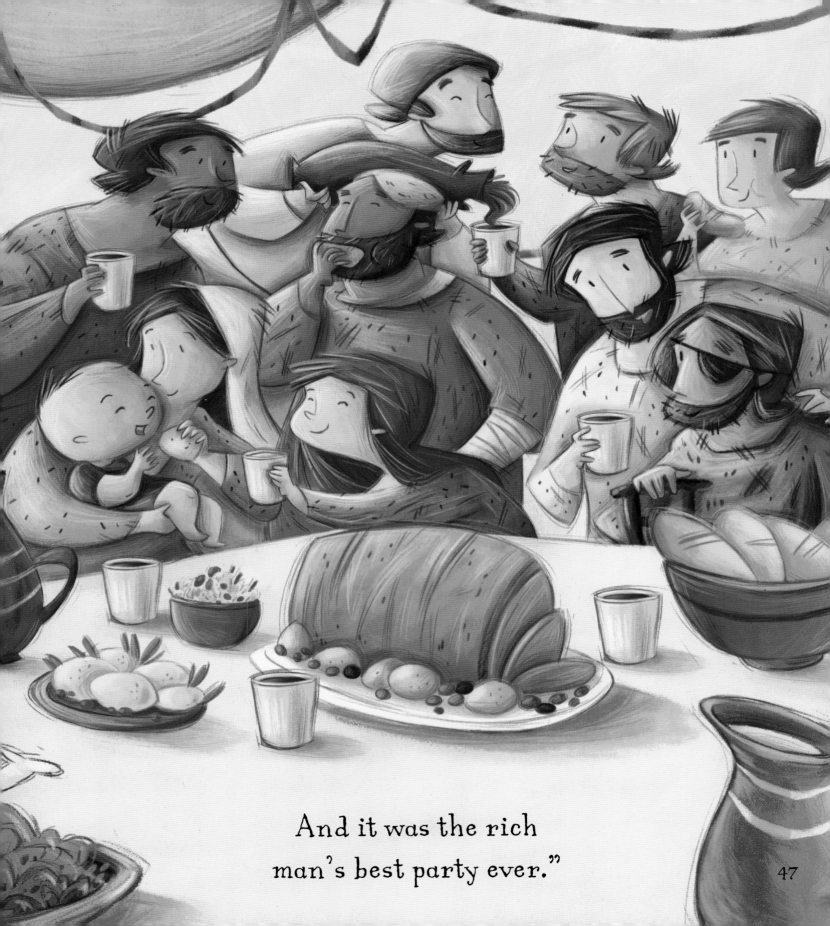

And it was the rich
man's best party ever."

"Everyone is invited to God's party in his heavenly kingdom," said Jesus.

"Anyone who puts God first will be made welcome."

"But people who don't make time for him may miss out on the feast."

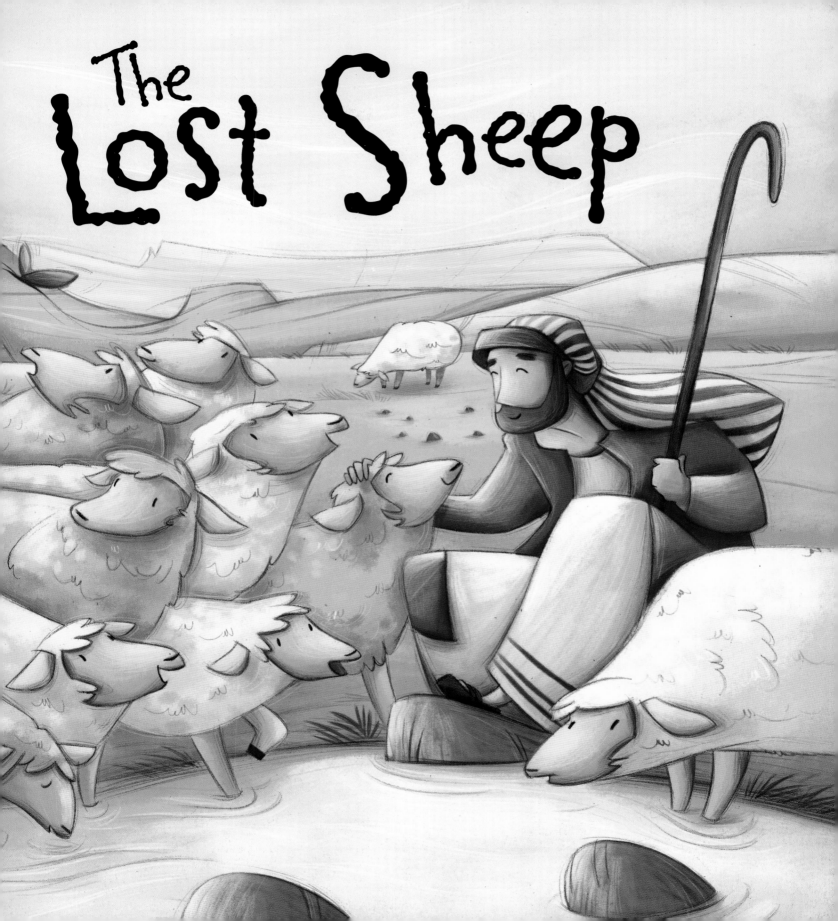

The Lost Sheep

All kinds of people came to listen to Jesus's stories.
Some were good. Some were bad. Jesus welcomed everyone.

One man asked, "Why do you spend so much time with bad people?"

Jesus told this story to explain...

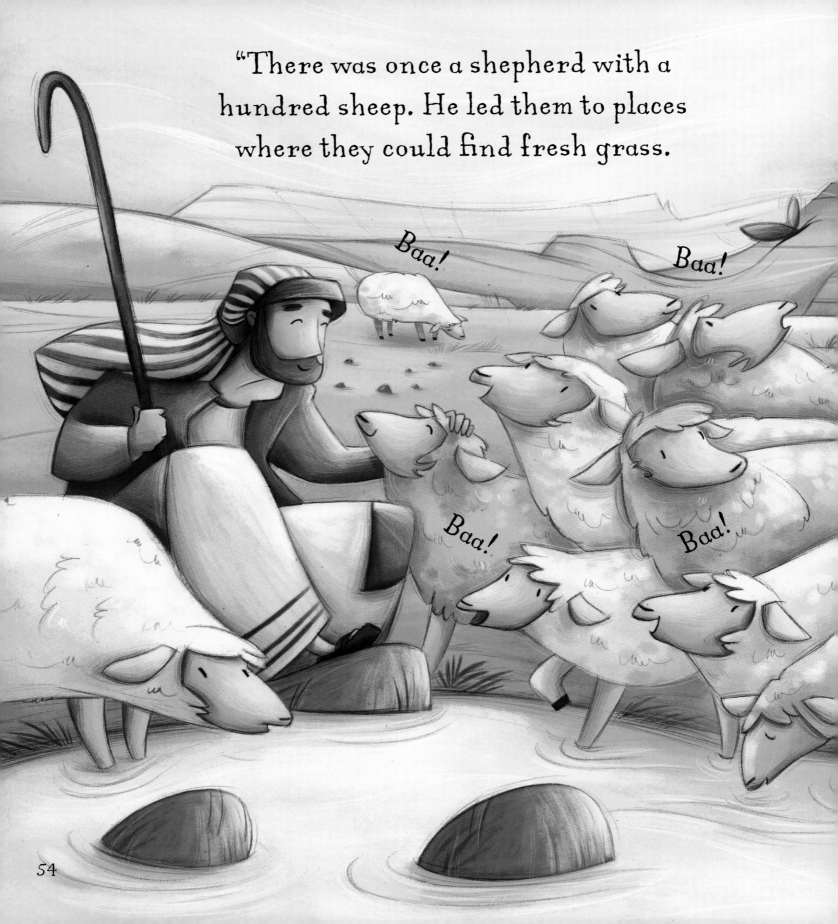

"There was once a shepherd with a hundred sheep. He led them to places where they could find fresh grass.

54

He made sure they always found water
to drink. He took great care of his flock.

Baa!

Baa!

55

"Every night, the shepherd counted all the sheep, making sure they were safe.

One night, he counted, as usual—all the way from one to ninety-nine.

But the last sheep was missing!

"One sheep must have wandered away and got lost.

The shepherd cared for the missing sheep as much as for the rest. He had to try to find the one that was lost.

58

He knew the ninety-nine sheep
would be safe together. So he set
out to look for the lost sheep.

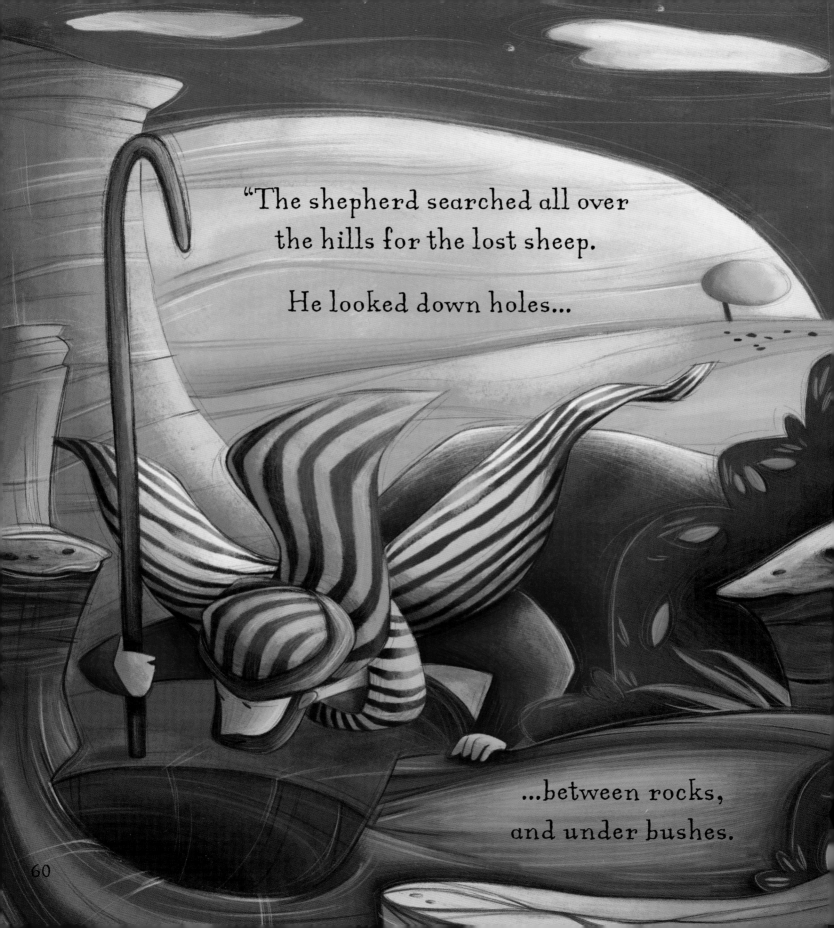

"The shepherd searched all over the hills for the lost sheep.

He looked down holes...

...between rocks, and under bushes.

60

Time passed and he didn't hear a bleat or a baa.

But the shepherd did not give up.

"At last, he heard a tiny sound.

"The shepherd was very happy.

He gently picked the sheep up.
He put it across his shoulders.

And he carried it all the way home.

"Then the shepherd called out to his friends:
'My sheep went astray and lost its way.
But now it's here, let's raise a cheer!'"

And they all had a party to celebrate."

"When you lose something precious,
aren't you pleased to find it?"
Jesus asked the people listening to him.

"That's just like God," he said.

"And that's why I spend time with people who have taken the wrong path and those who are in trouble."

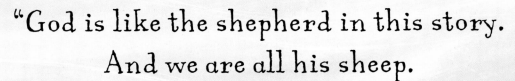

"God is like the shepherd in this story.
And we are all his sheep.

"When someone comes back to God, he is overjoyed. He doesn't want anyone to be lost."

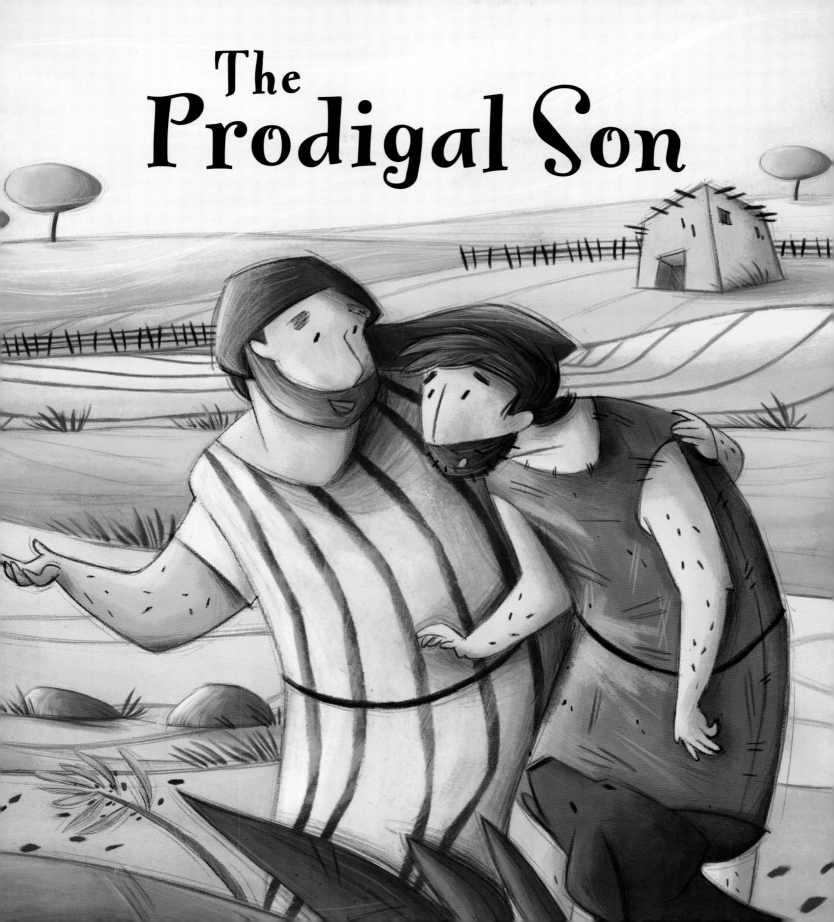

The Prodigal Son

One day, Jesus told this story to show that God forgives anyone who is sorry for doing wrong.

"There was a hardworking farmer who had a son. 'Half your money will be mine one day,' the son said to his father. 'Give it to me now.'

The farmer agreed and gave his son the money.

"The young man went far, far away.
He made lots of new friends.

Everyone enjoyed his parties.

He wasted his money having a good time.

77

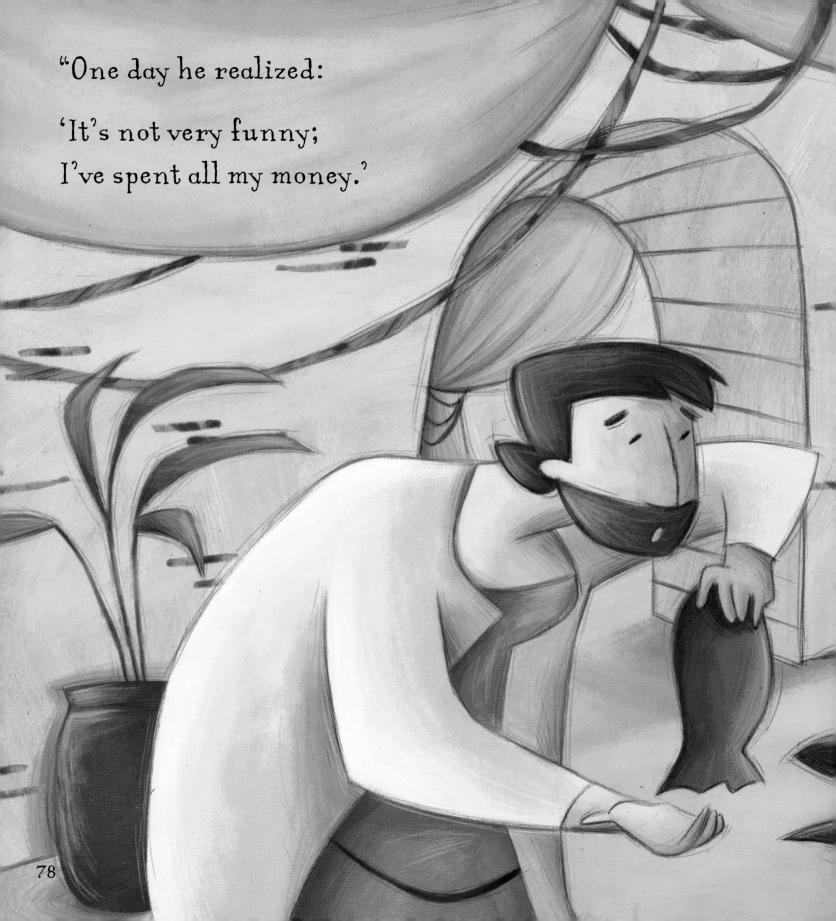

"One day he realized:

'It's not very funny;
I've spent all my money.'

78

All his friends had gone too.
He was alone and he was hungry.

The young man wasn't given much food.
He was always hungry.

"He thought, 'My father's servants live better than me.

Oink!

Snort!

'If I say sorry to my father, I could work for him. Then I would always have food to eat.'

"The young man set off
on the long journey home.

'I didn't treat
my father well,'
he thought.

'I must say sorry
to him. But he may not
welcome me home.'

85

"Later, he saw someone running toward him.

It was his father!

He had missed his son very much. He often watched for him and had seen him from far away.

He hugged and kissed the young man.

"'I'm sorry for doing wrong,' said the son.
'I am not fit to be called your son.
Can I be your servant?'

'Nonsense!' his father said. 'Welcome home!
We must celebrate your return.'

"His father told his servants to give the young man clean clothes and to prepare a great feast.

'My son was lost to me, but he has come back!' he said. 'We'll have a party to celebrate!'"

91

Jesus looked at the people around him.

"God is like that. If someone who has been bad changes and comes back to him, God forgives them and there is joy in heaven."

93

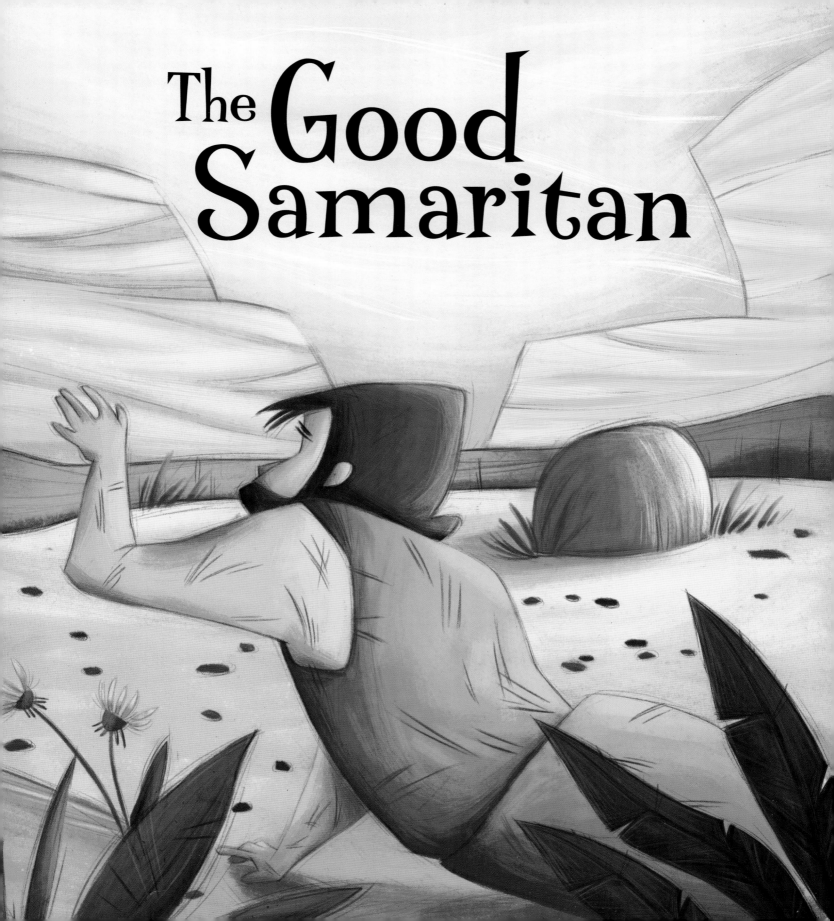

The Good Samaritan

One day, Jesus told this story to explain how
God wants people to care for one another.

"A man was walking from Jerusalem to Jericho.
He felt scared among the shadowy cliffs.
There might be wild animals in the rocky caves.

There might be...

97

"Robbers!

Suddenly, a gang of men jumped out
from their hiding place in the rocks.

98

The robbers knocked the man down. BASH! They beat him up and stole all he had. Then they left the poor man lying at the side of the road.

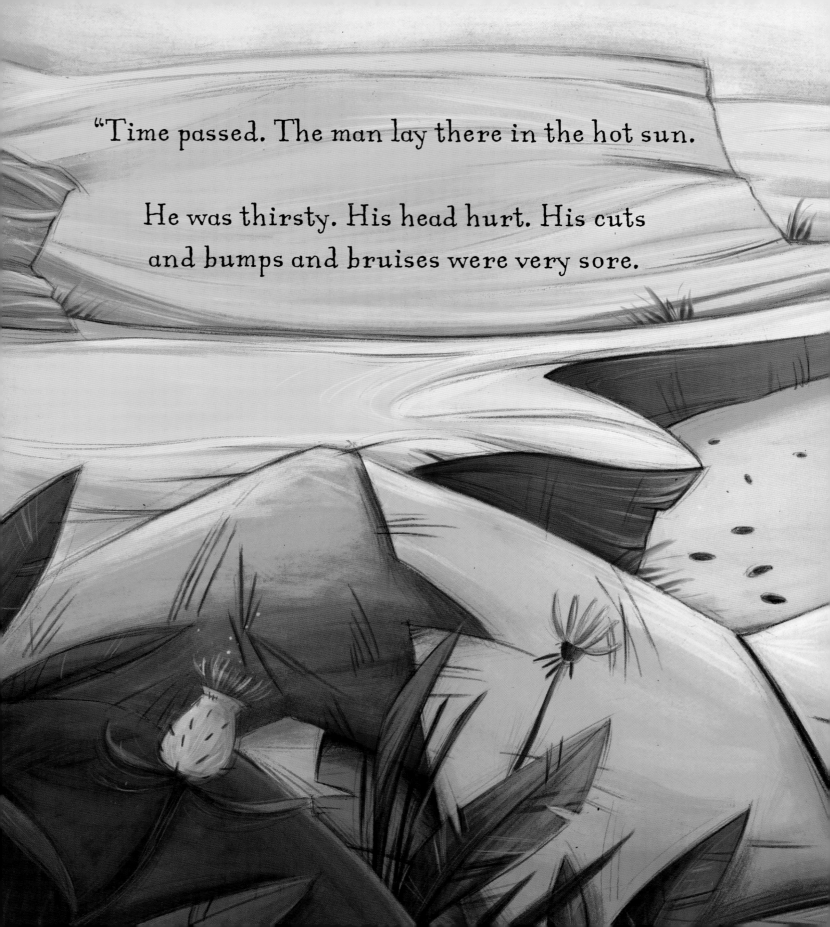

"Time passed. The man lay there in the hot sun.

He was thirsty. His head hurt. His cuts and bumps and bruises were very sore.

The man needed help.
How long would he have to wait?

"At last, the man heard footsteps.

'Help!'

A priest from the temple in Jerusalem came along. Surely this man who taught about God would stop to help?

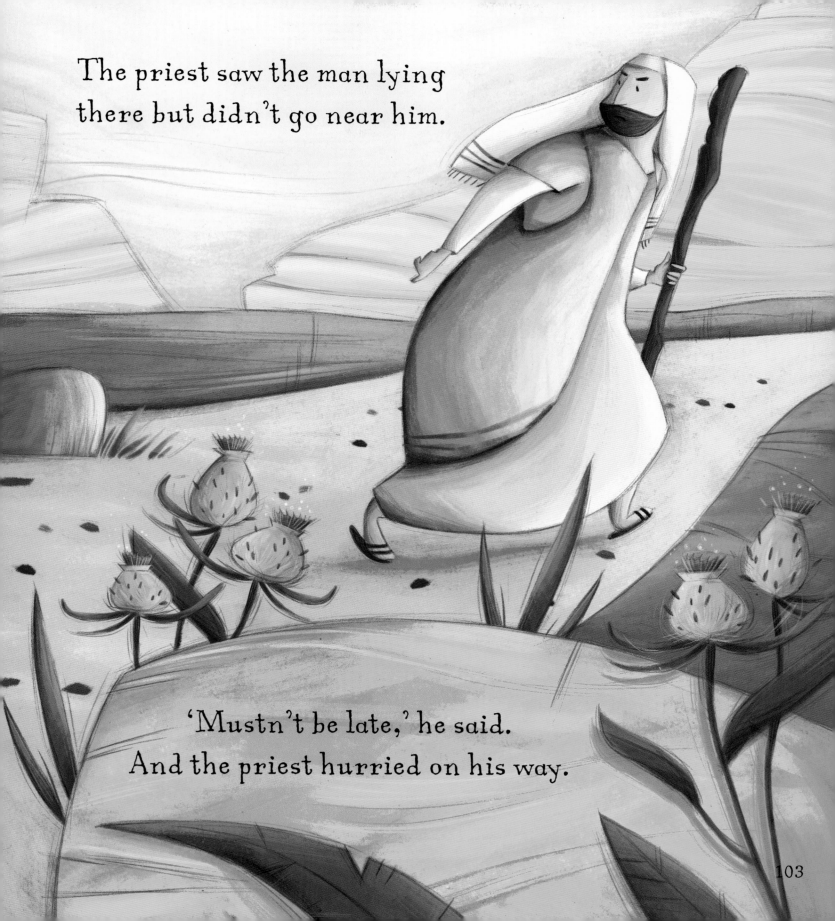

The priest saw the man lying there but didn't go near him.

'Mustn't be late,' he said.
And the priest hurried on his way.

"Later, the man heard more footsteps.

'Help!'

It was someone who helped
the priest in the temple.
Would he have time to stop?

104

He crept closer to look at the man. The man told him he had been attacked by robbers.

'The robbers might still be nearby!' he thought.

And he too went on his way.

Oh dear. It was a foreigner: a man from Samaria.
His people didn't talk to Samaritans.
They didn't like one another.

Why should this
stranger help?

"But the Samaritan stopped. He wasn't worried about being late or nasty robbers returning.

He gave the man a drink of water.
He bandaged the man's sore head. He
cleaned his cuts and bumps and bruises.

Then he gently lifted him onto his donkey.

"The Samaritan led the donkey down the rocky road until they reached an inn.

'I need somewhere to care for this poor man,' he told the innkeeper. 'He has been attacked by robbers.'

"The next day, the Samaritan gave the innkeeper some money and said:

'Take care of him and let him stay. If you need more, then I will pay.'

Promising he would return,
the Samaritan went on his way."

Jesus looked at the people
listening to his story.

"So which man did what
God wants?" he asked.

114

"The man who showed kindness,"
someone answered.

"Now go and do the same," said Jesus.
"Show God's love to anyone who needs
your help. Even strangers."

The Two Houses

Jesus wanted people to understand that listening to his words wasn't enough, they also had to live out his words each and every day.

So Jesus told this story...

"One day, a man decided to build a house.
'I've planned every detail,' he told his friend.

First, he bought a plot
of hard rocky ground.

119

He dug deep into the
earth above the rock.

It was hard work.

It was
hot work.

'A well-built house needs firm
foundations,' he told his friend.

121

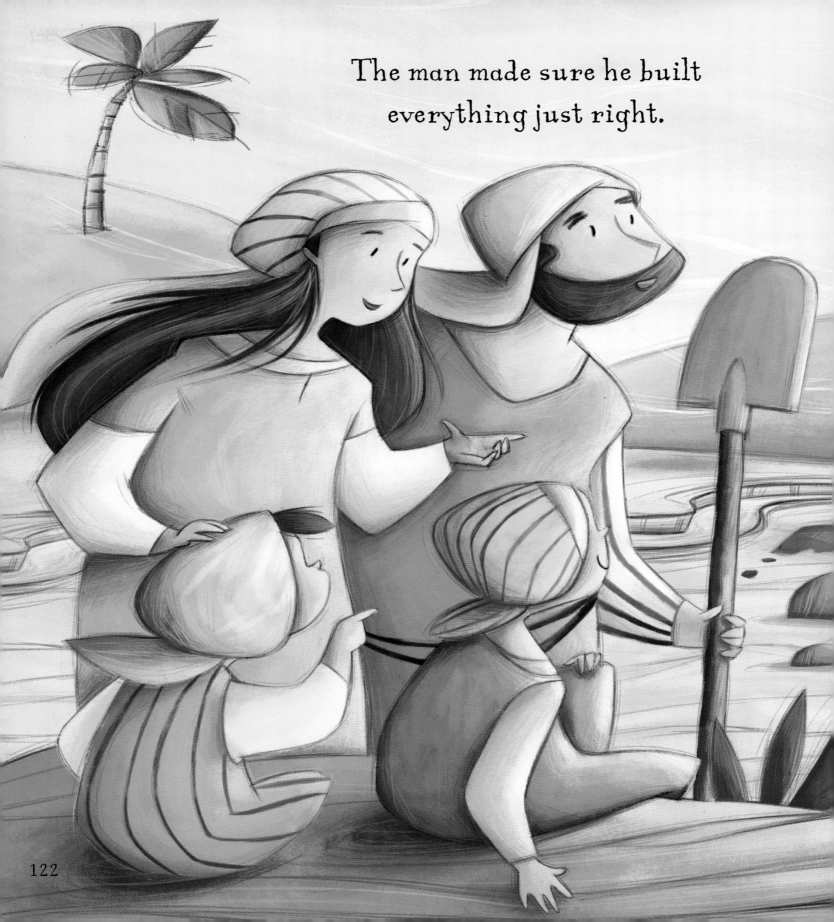

The man made sure he built
everything just right.

He was very pleased when at last
the house on the rock was finished.

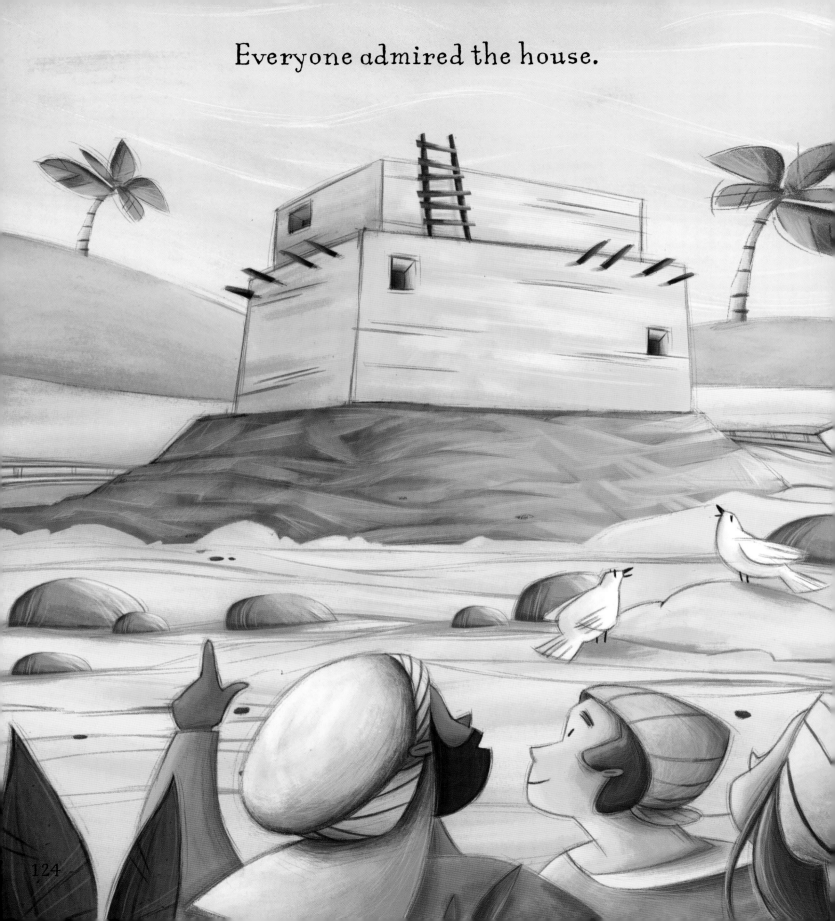

Everyone admired the house.

124

His friend even decided to build a new home of his own.
'There must be an easier place to build,' he thought.

His friend bought a plot of ground near the river.
It was soft and sandy and easy to dig.

'Building really
isn't such hard work,'
he thought.

Before long he, too, had finished building his house.

The two men were pleased
with their fine new homes.

Now they could enjoy the summer weather. And when winter came, the houses would keep them cozy and dry.

One day, dark clouds filled the sky.
Wind began to blow.

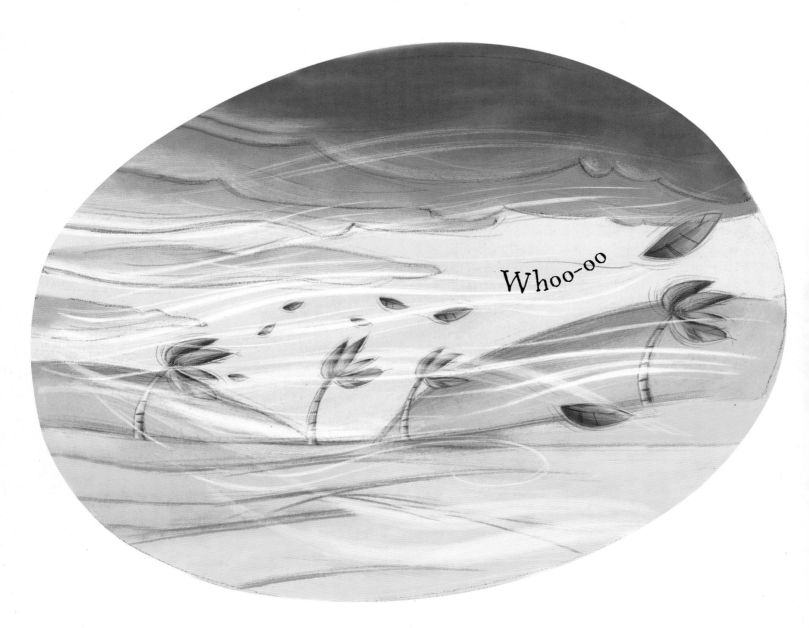

Rain fell, faster and faster.

Plip! Plop!

Water splashed over the sand.

Whenever wind whistled through the windows the house built on rock stood firm.

The house built on sand shook and shifted.
Its wobbly walls crumbled and lifted...

...until with a CRASH and a SPLASH the house built on sand fell down flat!"

Jesus looked at the people listening to his story.

"My words are like that rock," said Jesus.

"If you build your life on them you will stand firm too, as firm as the house on the rock."

NEXT STEPS

The Sower

What does Jesus want us to learn from the story of the Sower?

Jesus told this story to show that God wants people to open their hearts to him: to listen carefully to his words, think about what his words really mean and do what he asks. The seeds that fell on good, rich soil and grew well represent people who listen to God and act on his word.

You can find this story in Luke 8 in the Bible: "The seed is the word of God" (Luke 8:11).

Now that you've read the story, here are some things to talk about and join in with.

★ Have you ever planted any seeds? What happened to them?

★ Which seeds in this story grew big and strong?

★ Who did Jesus say the different seeds stood for?

★ What does Jesus want everyone to do?

★ Try to memorize this rhyme:

> "The little seeds fell here and there... the farmer didn't notice where."

★ Copy the actions of the characters in the story: pretend to walk up and down the field scattering seeds; chase away the greedy birds; help to gather the harvest.

The Great Feast

What does Jesus want us to learn from the story of the Great Feast?
Jesus wants people to understand that it's important to take God seriously. God has invited everyone to his kingdom but only people who put him first willbe able to join him.

You can find this story in Luke 14:15-24 in the Bible:
"Happy are those who will feast in God's kingdom" (Luke 14:15).

Now that you've read the story, here are some things to talk about and join in with.

★ How would you feel if a friend was too busy to come to your party?

★ What did the rich man do when his guests said they were too busy?

★ Why were the new guests surprised and happy to be invited?

★ Who do you think the rich man stands for?

★ Try to memorize the rich man's rhyme:

> "Anyone who wants to eat,
> let them come and take a seat."

★ Copy the actions of the characters in the story:
send out invitations; say you're too busy to come;
invite strangers to the party; look surprised to be
invited; enjoy the party.

The Lost Sheep

What does Jesus want us to learn from the story of the Lost Sheep?
Jesus wants people to understand God's love: he never gives up on people and
is overjoyed when anyone in trouble comes back to him, just as the shepherd
was overjoyed when he found his missing sheep.

You can find this story in Matthew 18 and Luke 15 in the Bible:
"There will be joy in heaven when someone comes back to God" (Luke 15:7).

**Now that you've read the story, here are some things to talk about
and join in with.**
* How many sheep were in the shepherd's flock?
* What did the shepherd do to care for his sheep?
* Why did the shepherd want to find the lost sheep?
* How did the shepherd take the sheep home?
* Why did the shepherd have a party?
* Try to memorize the shepherd's rhyme:
    "My sheep went astray and lost its way.
    But now it's here, let's raise a cheer!"
* Copy the actions of the shepherd: pretend
  to count the flock; search for the lost sheep;
  carry the sheep on your shoulders.

The Prodigal Son

What does Jesus want us to learn from the story of the Prodigal Son?
Jesus wants people to understand God's love and forgiveness: he never gives up on people. Just like the father in the story, God joyfully welcomes anyone who comes back to him.

You can find this story in Luke 15: 11-24 in the Bible:
"For this son of mine... was lost, and is found" (Luke 15:24).

Now that you've read the story, here are some things to talk about and join in with.
★ Do you think the father felt sad about what his son did?
★ What did the son expect to happen when he returned home?
★ What did the father do when his son said "Sorry"?
★ Who do you think the father stands for?
★ Try to memorize the son's rhyme:

> "It's not very funny;
> I've spent all my money."

★ Copy the actions of the characters in the story: pretend you're at a party; feed the pigs; watch for your son; give someone a big hug.

The Good Samaritan

What does Jesus want us to learn from the story of the Good Samaritan?
Jesus told this story to show how God wants us to treat other people. He wants us to be kind to others and to show love to anyone who needs help, just as the man from Samaria did when he stopped to help the injured traveler.

You can find this story in Luke 10 in the Bible:
"Love your neighbor as yourself" (Luke 10:27).

Now that you've read the story, here are some things to talk about and join in with.

* Say the names of some people you love: how have you ever helped them?
* Have you ever needed help?
* Were you helped by a person you knew?
* Does it make a difference whether we know the person we're helping or not?
* Try to memorize the Samaritan's rhyme:
    "Take care of him and let him stay.
    If you need more, then I will pay."
* Copy the actions of the characters in the story: pretend to walk down the road; care for the hurt man; pay the innkeeper; wave goodbye.

The Two Houses

What does Jesus want us to learn from the story of the Two Houses?

Jesus told this story to show how important it is to follow his example. Listening to his words and living God's way gives firm foundations for how to live, just as the rock provided strong foundations for the house.

You can find this story in Matthew 7 and Luke 6 in the Bible:
"Therefore everyone who hears these words of mine and puts them into practice is like a wise man who built his house on the rock" (Matthew 7:24).

Now that you've read the story, here are some things to talk about and join in with.

* Have you ever built anything? What did you use? How long did your creation last?
* How do you think builders decide where to build a house?
* Why is rock good to build on?
* What does Jesus want people to build their lives on?
* Try to memorize the rhyme:
    "The house built on sand shook and shifted.
    Its wobbly walls crumbled and lifted..."

* Copy the actions of the two men: pretend to dig; lay bricks; pick leaves; try to keep dry in the rain and rising water.